GARDEN GUIDES

THE FLOWER GARDEN

GARDEN GUIDES

THE FLOWER GARDEN

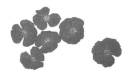

LANCE HATTATT

Illustrations by
ELAINE FRANKS

A Siena book.
Siena is an imprint of Parragon Books.

This edition first published in 1996 by
Parragon Book Service Ltd
Unit 13–17, Avonbridge Trading Estate
Atlantic Road
Avonmouth
Bristol BS11 9QD

Produced by
Robert Ditchfield Ltd
Combe Court
Kerry's Gate
Hereford HR2 0AH

ISBN 0 75251 610 8

A copy of the British Library Cataloguing in Publication Data is
available from the Library.

Typeset by Action Typesetting Ltd, Gloucester
Colour origination by Mandarin Offset Ltd, Hong Kong
Printed and bound in Italy

ACKNOWLEDGEMENTS
Most of the photographs were taken in the author's garden, Arrow Cottage, Ledgemoor, Weobley. The publishers
would also like to thank the many people and organizations who have allowed photographs to be taken for this
book, including the following:

Lucinda Aldrich-Blake; Polly Bolton, Nordybank Nurseries, Clee St Margaret; Burford House, Tenbury Wells;
Lallie Cox, Woodpeckers, Marlcliff, Bidford-on-Avon; Katharina Turner; Mr and Mrs K. Dawson, Chennels Gate,
Eardisley; Dinmore Manor; Richard Edwards, Well Cottage, Blakemere; Great Dixter; Haseley Court; The Hon
Mrs Peter Healing, The Priory, Kemerton; Hergest Croft; Mrs Daphne Hoskins, Kellaways; Mrs David Lewis, Ash
Farm, Much Birch; Mrs Richard Paice, Bourton House; Pentwyn Cottage Garden, Bacton; The Picton Garden,
Colwall; Powis Castle (National Trust); Royal Botanic Gardens, Kew; RHS Garden, Wisley; Sissinghurst Castle
(National Trust); Stone House Cottage, Kidderminster; Raymond Treasure, Stockton Bury Farm, Kimbolton; Mrs
Geoffrey Williams, Close Farm, Crockham Hill; Mrs David Williams-Thomas, The Manor House, Birlingham;
Wakehurst Place (National Trust); York Gate, Leeds.

Photographs of the following plants are reproduced by kind permission of Thompson & Morgan Ltd., Ipswich,
Suffolk: *Salvia splendens*, Sweet Pea 'Maggie May'.

CONTENTS

POISONOUS PLANTS

In recent years, concern has been voiced about poisonous plants or plants which can cause allergic reactions if touched. The fact is that many plants are poisonous, some in a particular part, others in all their parts. For the sake of safety, it is always, without exception, essential to assume that no part of a plant should be eaten unless it is known, without any doubt whatsoever, that the plant or its part is edible and that it cannot provoke an allergic reaction in the individual person who samples it. It must also be remembered that some plants can cause severe dermatitis, blistering or an allergic reaction if touched, in some individuals and not in others. It is the responsibility of the individual to take all the above into account.

How to Use This Book

Where appropriate, approximate measurements of a plant's height have been given, and also the spread where this is significant, in both metric and imperial measures. The height is the first measurement, as for example 1.2m × 60cm/4 × 2ft. However, both height and spread vary so greatly from garden to garden since they depend on soil, climate and position, that these measurements are offered as guides only. This is especially true of trees and shrubs where ultimate growth can be unpredictable.

The following symbols are also used throughout the book:
    ○ = thrives best or only in full sun
    ◑ = thrives best or only in part-shade
    ● = succeeds in full shade
    E = evergreen

Where no sun symbol and no reference to sun or shade is made in the text, it can be assumed that the plant tolerates sun or light shade.

Plant Names

For ease of reference this book gives the botanical name under which a plant is most widely listed for the gardener. These names are sometimes changed and in such cases the new name has been included. Common names are given wherever they are in frequent use.

The Flower Garden

EVERYONE LOVES A FLOWER GARDEN. For it is here that a multitude of delightful and lovely plants can be brought together into a picturesque whole. The combining of colour, the consideration of form and the appreciation of texture will all contribute to harmonious and pleasing flower borders.

SHAPING THE BORDERS

Traditionally borders mark the edge of a lawn, follow the line of a path or front an adjacent feature such as a wall, hedge or fence. Today the name also applies to free-standing or island beds as well as those which encompass sweeps and curves.

For a formal effect, symmetrically shaped borders of squares, rectangles and circles are best. Thought should be given to proportion and, ideally, one border will be matched by another of equal size and shape.

This is very confident use of colour whereby brilliant effects have been achieved through combining hues at the hot end of the scale – gold, burnt orange and ruby – toned down by the sombre purple-brown of foliage. The shapes of the group are also interesting. The flat flower heads of the achillea at the rear contrast with the sword leaves of the crocosmia.

In cool, moist part-shade, *Primula florindae* (Giant cowslip) rises above orange mimulus.

POSITIONING PLANTS

Border preparation is essential if flowering plants are to perform well. Following the removal of all perennial weeds and coarse grasses, the ground should be well dug to incorporate plenty of organic matter. Heavy or poorly drained soil may be improved by the addition of well rotted compost, sharp sand, bonfire ash or horticultural grit.

Container-grown plants allow planting at virtually any time although extremes of weather should be avoided. It is worth taking trouble when planting to give plants the best possible start. For this a good-sized hole needs to be dug to which should be added mature compost. Once removed from their pots, plants should be placed to a depth which corresponds with the original soil mark. Where a strong root system exists, roots may be gently teased out before filling in the hole and firming round to eliminate any air pockets. A thorough watering should then be given.

The way in which a border faces, the aspect, and the amount of sun or shade it receives has a bearing on what will grow. An open, sunny site with some shelter at the rear is ideal for many sun-loving plants. Shade, cast by a canopy of tree leaves, from which there may well be 'drip', prevents certain plants from flourishing.

The degree of alkalinity or acidity of the soil, measured on a pH scale, determines what will thrive. A pH of 7.0 indicates a neutral soil, above is alkaline, below acid. Some plants will not tolerate lime and will only succeed on acid soils with a low pH. Others demand more alkaline conditions.

Borders made up of generous curves, with an absence of straight lines, can give an illusion of space. Island beds create a softening impression and serve to break the monotony of a large area.

Personal preference, taste and the requirements of the site will all determine layout. Certainly the final arrangement will take into account the need to show plants to their best possible advantage.

Wallflowers in mingled shades of buttery yellow and dark red are a scented addition to a patio.

The spotted leopard lily (*Lilium pardalinum*) produces its turkscap flowers in summer.

Lilium 'King Pete', a robust low-growing lily, also flowers in summer. It will do well in a large pot which can be placed on a terrace or even positioned in a bed.

THEMES AND SCHEMES

Winter lends itself to the job of border planning when the days are short and outside activities are curtailed. Plant catalogues and seed lists are excellent sources to be pored over and from which selections may be made. By drawing out the flower border to scale, and plotting the position of plants, a pleasing and successful display is guaranteed.

Colour planning is a matter of personal choice. In a small garden a mixed-colour border may be preferred where plants are chosen as much for height and spread and flowering period as for colour. A blaze of brightly coloured plants may well appeal with strong reds placed alongside brilliant yellows. Alternatively the combination of pastel shades creates a subtle, tranquil effect. Where space permits, single-colour borders can give an air of sophistication. However, no scheme should be adhered to too rigidly for very often the introduction of another single colour serves to highlight and intensify the principal colour. The flowers of a blue border are made more special when set against a foil of silver and grey leaves. A yellow arrangement of lemons through to deep gold, complemented by variegated foliage, is a bright scheme for a dreary day. The introduction of white, or mid blue, enhances the design.

If room allows, blocks of plants of a single variety placed together make an immediate

11

The classic well-loved combination of the tulip 'China Pink' and forget-me-nots.

THE FLOWERS

Mixing together annuals, biennials, perennials and bulbs in the flower borders will give colour and interest for the greater part of the year.

A hardy annual completes its life cycle in one year. Grown from seed it will germinate, flower, set seed and die within a single season. Seeds are usually sown in the open ground in the spring. Half-hardy annuals behave in exactly the same manner but the seed needs to be sown under cover. Young plants are set out when the threat of frosts is past.

In contrast a biennial requires two seasons. During the first it will produce stems and leaves, delaying flowering until the second when it too will set seed and die.

Perennial plants will establish and remain in the border for a number of years. As a general rule they make new growth in the spring, flower, then die down in the winter. Not all are totally hardy and some may not survive severe weather conditions. Others are evergreen and so do not completely disappear.

Bulbs and corms and tubers consist of fleshy organs which, when planted, will grow for many seasons.

PLANT CARE

Weeding the borders in the early part of the year results in much labour saved later on. Where possible the application of a mulch, some form of organic matter, to a depth of about 7.5cm/3in promotes healthy and vigorous plants. Additionally, a mulch reduces water evaporation during dry periods. As flowers develop, a liquid feed may be applied.

impact. Planted in groups of threes, fives, sevens or more, such an arrangement ensures flowers, and therefore interest, over a long period. As an alternative, set clumps of the same plant to flower in informal drifts. The repetition of a particular flower, a spot plant, adds unity to the scheme and carries the eye forward.

(*Above*) *Penstemon* 'Edithiae' is low-growing, bushy and in flower from spring to early summer. Although unfussy about soil conditions, it prefers full sun. Stocks can be readily increased by taking cuttings in the later part of the year.

The shrub *Lavatera* 'Burgundy Wine' is visible through an airy haze of *Verbena bonariensis* which is a marvellous plant for the front of a border as it adds interest and is see-through. It self-seeds gently and doesn't need staking.

For this purpose a wide range of fertilizers is available. Manufacturers' instructions should be followed exactly.

As plants begin to grow, those of less robust habit will need some form of staking to protect them from wind and rain. For lower-growing, smaller plants it is sufficient to drive in three or four sticks around the plant and tie these with string. Hazel or birch twigs are ideal for this. Taller, stronger-growing specimens require a more substantial approach of bamboo canes or manufactured stakes. These should be put in place early in the season; further staking and tying may be necessary at intervals.

Unfortunately, periodically flowers are attacked by pests, virus or fungal disease. The nature and intensity of any attack will vary from season to season. Where diseases are detected at an early stage and treatment carried out, control is relatively easy. In many instances, particularly in the case of pests, Nature herself will take charge. It must be remembered that not all insects are harmful in the garden. Many are not only harmless but helpful.

1. EARLY SPRING

Thoughts of winter are set aside as the first buds burst. Fragile flowers announce the start of a new season.

FIRST FLOWERS

PERHAPS NOTHING IS MORE WELCOME in the garden than the first sightings of spring flowers to mark the end of the drab days of winter.

A small jug of blooms from the early spring garden dominated by the delicate violet petals of *Iris unguicularis* (Algerian iris).

Winter-flowering heathers provide bold clumps of glowing colour throughout early spring. They thrive in well drained soil.

◆ *Heathers should be clipped hard back as the flowers die. Fresh foliage will soon emerge.*

***Galanthus* 'Magnet'** This snowdrop's tiny flowers stand proud above grey-green sword-like leaves to brave the worst of weather. ◑, ● 10cm/4in

PLANNING AHEAD

Now is the time to order seeds of annuals for summer displays.

Sow half-hardy annuals under glass to plant out when the threat of frost is past.

Hardy annuals may be sown directly into well prepared seed-beds where they are to bloom.

Cyclamen coum is available in many different forms. Leaves are often interestingly marbled. ◑, 10cm/4in

◆ *Cyclamen are ideal subjects for dry situations where little else will grow.*

Snowdrops are ideally grown in a woodland situation
although they will prosper in cool, moist soil at the base
of a sunless wall. Here they look splendid in contrast to
the deep red leaves of bergenia.

◆ *Division of snowdrops should take place after
flowering but before the foliage has died down.*

FIRST FLOWERS

EARLY SPRING BULBS come into their own at this time of year to provide warmth and cheer to the borders. Most are suited to growing under deciduous trees and shrubs where, later in the year, their dying foliage will be concealed. With careful planning it is possible to have a succession of bulbs in flower.

Crocus are amongst the most versatile of bulbs. Grow in the border or in pots, in sun or in shade.

◆ *Mature bulbs should be planted about 5cm/2in deep and 10cm/4in apart.*

Anemone blanda is a plant for the edge of woodland. Its many petalled blooms are usually of mid-blue. 10 cm/4in

Crocus tommasinianus should be placed in drifts in an open position and left undisturbed to naturalize. 10cm/4in

Chionodoxa luciliae The common name, Glory of the Snow, well describes these pretty bluish-lilac flowers. 10cm/4in

Primula denticulata The drumstick primula is happiest in moisture-retentive soil. ◑, 20 × 30cm/8in × 1ft

Narcissus bulbocodium
Long trumpets of clear yellow distinguish this early flowering, small daffodil. ○, 15–20cm/6–8in

Narcissus cyclamineus is particularly distinctive with its protruding trumpet and reflexed perianth segments. 15–20cm/6–8in

***Narcissus* 'February Gold'**
This miniature daffodil enjoys damp soil and is an excellent choice for rough grass. 15–20cm/6–8in

***Narcissus* 'Tête-à-Tête'** A robust little hybrid which produces more than one flower on each stem. Provided with good drainage, it makes a worthwhile choice for a terracotta pot. 15–20cm/6–8in

***Iris reticulata* 'Harmony'**
This blue iris is an early flowering dwarf form for a sunny position. 10–15cm/4–6in

◆ *Propagate the reticulata irises by lifting and dividing the bulbs in late summer.*

FIRST FLOWERS

POT PLANTS

Many of the small spring bulbs are ideally suited to be grown in pots or as additions to sink gardens. Ensure plenty of drainage by placing several crocks at the bottom of the pot. Plant in suitable growing compost to which has been added a good measure of horticultural grit. A light dressing of a low nitrogen fertilizer in autumn and early spring will ensure healthy growth.

STARTING *in* STYLE

Iris unguicularis Place the Algerian iris in a pot to stand beside an entrance or doorway for its brief but lovely flowering period. E, ☾, 20 × 60cm/ 8in × 2ft

CULTIVATING HELLEBORES

Hellebores enjoy rich conditions. An annual mulch of well rotted compost or a liberal application of leaf mould will be beneficial.

As the flowers of *Helleborus orientalis* (Lenten rose) unfold, remove all the previous year's leaves. This makes for a tidier plant and shows off the flowers to good effect.

Euphorbia rigida Glaucous leaves make this a most striking spurge to be grown in a sunny position. ◯, E, 60 × 45cm/ 1 × 1½ft

♦ Euphorbias are poisonous plants. Contact with skin may cause irritation.

***Helleborus foetidus* 'Wester Flisk'** has greyish-green leaves with distinctive, red-tinged flower stalks. E, ◑, 45 × 45cm/1½ × 1½ft

No spring border should be without aristocratic hellebores, lovely early-flowering iris or the majestic spurge, *Euphorbia rigida*. In a period of the year when the weather is often discouraging, these flowers transform the garden, bringing to it both colour and interest.

It is not simply the range of hues from purest white to deepest black, but the limitless variations of shading, veining and spotting that make *Helleborus orientalis* such magical plants.

SHADE LOVERS

As SPRING UNFOLDS, the sun's rays reach down through the bare branches of trees to bosky clearings where life begins to stir. Before they are overshadowed by a canopy of leaves, early plants burst into flower.

Primula **'Dusky Lady'** Dark and mysterious, this deeply coloured primula has a long flowering season. 15 × 15cm/6 × 6in

Epimedium × *youngianum* **'Roseum'** From a base of attractive leaves rise stems of tiny rose-coloured flowers. 25 × 30cm/10in × 1ft

Epimedium × *youngianum* **'Niveum'** Small white flowers are eye-catching in the early part of the year. 25 × 30cm/10in × 1ft

Primula **'Hose-in-Hose'** Unusual for flowering above a tiny ruff of leaves. 10 × 10cm/4 × 4in

Omphalodes cappadocica **'Cherry Ingram'** Early on, this is a reluctant flowerer. Later it will be a mass of blue. 15 × 30cm/6in × 1ft

Hugging the floor of the woodland, the winter aconite vies with the snowdrop to be amongst the first flowers of spring. Its glossy, bright yellow buttercup flowers, overtopping a ruff of deeply cut leaves, will make a splash of gold year after year if left undisturbed. The little blue *Iris histroides*, 10cm/4in tall, blooms slightly later.

Leucojum vernum
Sometimes known as the spring snowflake. The bell-shaped flower of six petals is tipped green.
20 × 10cm/8 × 4in

SHADE
LOVERS

Euphorbia amygdaloides var. robbiae Bracts rather than flowers characterize this spurge for dry conditions. 75 × 75 cm/2½ × 2½ft

Scilla mischtschenkoana (S. tubergeniana) Flowers of a fragile blue to enliven an otherwise dull corner. 10 × 7.5cm/4 × 3in

Vinca minor 'Burgundy' An exceptional coloured form of the spreading lesser periwinkle in bloom from mid-spring to autumn. 15 × 60cm+/6in × 2ft+

Anemone apennina The blue flowers of this pretty species become flattened stars in the spring sun. 10 × 7.5cm/4 × 3in

◆ *Grow erythroniums amongst apennine anemones for a sparkling carpet of bloom.*

Cardamine trifolia This delicate little lady's smock delights with tiny flowers of pink or white. 20 × 30cm/8in x 1ft

SHEETS OF WOOD ANEMONE in the wild are one of the delights of springtime. A little too vigorous for the small garden, they rapidly increase by creeping rhizomes to form large pools of white. Placed alongside some of the early flowering narcissus they work well under leafless shrubs.

***Cardamine pratensis* 'Flore Pleno'** A very pretty double flower which has been in cultivation for several centuries. 20 × 30cm/ 8in × 1ft

***Anemone nemorosa* 'Bowles' Purple'** is one of a number of cultivated forms of wood anemone. 15 × 30cm/6in × 1ft

◆ *Anemone nemorosa* 'Robinsoniana' *has lavender-blue flowers and may be more easily obtainable.*

2. SPRING

*All the promise of the gardening year
is encapsulated in the cheerful blooms
of spring.*

MASSED EFFECTS

DAFFODILS ANNOUNCE THE ARRIVAL OF SPRING. Whether in the wild or in the garden their assertive trumpets capture the imagination and bring cheer to the darkest of days.

Narcissus poeticus The pheasant's eye is beautifully scented. ◐, 45cm/1½ft

◆ *Remove dead heads after flowering but leave foliage to die down.*

Narcissus 'Ice Follies' Opening pale lemon yellow, this daffodil gradually ages to white. 45cm/1½ft

Narcissus 'Hawera' Many bulbs are well suited to growing in gravel. Here 'Hawera' enjoys the good drainage. 45cm/1½ft

Muscari neglectum Dense spikes of blue typify the grape hyacinth which is tolerant of most situations. 10–15cm/4–6in

Brunnera macrophylla (Siberian bugloss) Forget-me-not type flowers above good green foliage. ◑, 45 × 45cm/1½ × 1½ft

Aubrieta deltoidea A carpeter to spill over walls or paths. Cut back hard after flowering. ○, 5 × 45cm/2in × 1½ft

Myosotis No spring border should be without the much loved forget-me-not. Allow it to seed at will. 15 × 30cm/6in × 1ft

BULB CARE

For spring flowering, plant bulbs during the previous autumn.

As a broad guide bulbs should be planted to at least twice their depth.

Most bulbs may be allowed to remain in the ground although tulips and hyacinths may, if desired, be lifted once the leaves have died down.

An annual dressing of bonemeal lightly forked in before bulbs commence flowering will help to maintain vigour.

Saxifraga × urbium The common London pride should not be despised for it is the most serviceable of plants. 30 × 30cm/1 × 1ft

Alyssum saxatile will brighten the rock garden with its yellow flowers. ○, 15 × 30cm/6in × 1ft

Arabis caucasica A profusion of white flowers over evergreen foliage. Good for difficult spots. 15 × 30cm/6in × 1ft

A white spring bed dominated by grouped planting of the impressive tulip 'Purissima' with white honesty and primroses.

◆ *Note the effect of repeat plantings of bold subjects.*

MASSED EFFECTS

BULBS FOR SHOW

Spring bulbs massed together are a joy to behold. For a stunning, continuous display, plant large quantities of one kind together. This avoids a spotted effect.

Choose bulbs with varying flower times. This will provide for a succession of colour over a long period.

Position bulbs amongst shrubs which will flower later to provide immediate interest and to extend the season.

Doronicum columnae Leopard's bane is an old-fashioned garden plant which continues to perform well. 45 × 45cm/1½ × 1½ft

Ranunculus Cultivated forms of celandine are well worth growing for their spring cheer. 10cm/4in

Cheiranthus The heady fragrance of wallflowers is one of the many joys of spring. 30 × 30cm/1 × 1ft

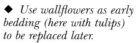

◆ *Use wallflowers as early bedding (here with tulips) to be replaced later.*

Phlox subulata This evergreen mound-former will gradually spread outwards to carpet the ground. ○, 20cm/8in

Polyanthus These cheerful spring flowers are a delight when planted closely in semi-shade. 15cm/6in

Ajuga reptans 'Catlin's Giant' is a fine form of bugle with a metallic shine to the purple leaves. E, 15 × 60cm/6in × 2ft

TULIPS UNDERPLANTED WITH FORGET-ME-NOTS is a tried and tested marriage which never fails to please. The mix of bright colours captures the popular style of a cottage garden. Choosing a single variety of tulip, rather than different forms, will elevate the scheme to something rather special.

Here the new shoots of crocosmia provide a contrast of form and texture to the mass of forget-me-nots.

Tulipa '**China Pink**' A graceful lily-flowered tulip of pure satin pink with a white base. ○, 45cm/1½ft

Tulipa '**West Point**' Used in a planting with brunnera, the elegant, lemon-yellow flowers of the tulips contrast with the clear blue of the brunnera. ○, 45cm/1½ft

◆ *A good form of brunnera is 'Langtrees' with silver spotting on the leaves.*

SOMETHING UNUSUAL

THE CHOICE OF PLANTS AVAILABLE for the spring borders is limitless and no-one would be without many of the garden-worthy stalwarts which provide such promise at this time of year. The inclusion of something a little different adds certain style and transforms the conventional into the dramatic.

MAINTAINING APPEARANCES

Warmer days and the season's rain showers will produce many weed seedlings. Removing them now will be time well spent. In closely planted areas use a handfork. In more open ground a hoe will make light work of this task.

Dead-head spent flowers to prolong the flowering period and to keep plants looking good.

In dry periods water young plants to help them establish. Avoid surface watering. Water should be sufficient to penetrate the root system.

Uvularia grandiflora The bellwort prefers moist peaty soil. A most graceful spring plant. ◐, 30 × 30cm/1 × 1ft

Mertensia virginica A most appealing plant which is seldom seen. By mid-summer it has died down completely. ◐, 60 × 45cm/ 2 × 1½ft

***Ipheion uniflorum* 'Wisley Blue'** Starry blue flowers are an enchanting addition to the front of the border. 15cm/6in

Erythronium dens-canis is but one of many dog's tooth violets enjoying a semi-shaded, humus rich situation. 15cm/6in

***Pulmonaria* 'Bowles' Blue'** A beautiful lungwort and one of many available forms. ◑, 30 × 45cm/ 1 × 1½ft

***Dicentra* 'Bacchanal'** is an exceptionally deep red bleeding heart with finely cut, glaucous green leaves. 30 × 30cm/1 × 1ft

Lysichiton americanus Yellow spathes and broad leaves are a feature of the moisture-loving skunk cabbage. 60 × 75cm/2 × 2½ft

Fritillaria imperialis The crown imperial is one of the most majestic of garden plants and well worth growing. ○, 1m × 30cm/ 3 × 1ft

***Sanguinaria canadensis* 'Plena'** Unhappily the flowers of this marvellous little plant do not last for long. ◑, 10cm/4in

Camassia leichtlinii requires plenty of moisture when in growth. Effective near water or in grass. 75 × 30cm/ 2½ × 1ft

***Darmera peltata* (Umbrella plant)** flowers from creeping rhizomes before the glossy leaves appear. 1m × 60cm/ 3 × 2ft

WOODLANDS ARE THE NATURAL HOME for many of our best loved spring plants. The early primroses, wood anemones and wild daffodils, later followed with sheets of bluebells, capture the very essence of the season. Not surprisingly many of these plants have been brought into garden cultivation. Even in a limited space it is possible to create the right growing environment in a garden setting for these woodlanders.

Primula veris To thrive the cowslip should be grown in grass in an open situation where it can benefit from full sun. Yellow flowers are often tinged orange or red. 20cm/8in

◆ *Less common in cultivation is the oxlip,* Primula elatior.

In the WILD

Scilla non-scripta Bluebells should mainly be reserved for the wild garden where, left undisturbed, they will naturalize. ◑ , 25cm/10in

BLUEBELLS AND POPPIES

For a really dashing scheme, plant bluebells with the yellow, and sometimes orange, Welsh poppy, *Meconopsis cambrica*. Both will increase readily from self-sown seed.

Pulsatilla vulgaris Several colour forms of the pasque flower are in cultivation. All require good drainage. 30 × 30cm/1 × 1ft

Viola odorata The leaves often tend to overpower the wonderfully scented, dainty flowers of the sweet violet. 10 × 30cm/4in × 1ft

Primula 'Valley Red' Primulas are an attractive addition to the less formal parts of the garden. ◑ , 30 × 30cm/1 × 1ft

Caltha palustris A good choice for a damp spot beside a pond or stream. ◑ , 60 × 60cm/2 × 2ft

Cardamine pratensis The lady's smock is to be found growing in damp meadows and ditches in the wild. ◑ , 25cm/10in

Galium odoratum The sweet woodruff is a pleasing little carpeter with tiny, white star flowers for light shade. 20 × 30cm/8in × 1ft

Primula vulgaris A cool shady bank makes an ideal site in which to place clumps of primroses. 10cm/4in

Meconopsis cambrica Allowed to seed around, the Welsh poppy will lend a casual air to the garden. 30 × 30cm/1 × 1ft

Convallaria majalis Beautifully scented, lily-of-the-valley will gradually increase over the years. ◑ , ● , 20cm/8in

FLOWERING ALPINE MEADOWS are a source of inspiration. The impression of wild flowers sprinkled amongst gently waving grasses is something to be desired and, if possible, copied. However, achieving a balance of flowers and grass is not always easy.

Fritillaria meleagris The exciting spotting on the bell flower has given rise to the name snakeshead.
◑ , 25cm/10in

◆ *These flowers are excellent for grouping in a shady border or for naturalizing in grass.*

3. EARLY SUMMER

*Beautiful flowers, fresh foliage and
longer, warmer days combine to make
this one of the loveliest of times.*

COMBINING PLANTS

AS SUMMER GATHERS PACE so the borders begin to fill out. Soft, pastel colours predominate and it is the arrangement of these which determines the success or otherwise of the planting schemes.

Giving careful thought to the placing of flowers (here, *Viola cornuta* and *Malva moschata alba*) will result in effects which are pleasing to the eye and which strike chords of harmony throughout the garden.

***Delphinium* 'Alice Artindale'** One of the loveliest of all delphiniums, 'Alice Artindale' possesses the most sumptuous double flowers. Place it with violet, green, even some reds. ○, 1.5m × 75cm/5 × 2½ft

Delphiniums, feverfew, salvia, viola and mallow are combined and this restful arrangement of yellow and blue tints, where the most prevalent colour is the green of the foliage, works well. The addition of tones of orange or violet would make for a less relaxed, more startling picture.

COMBINING PLANTS

EXCITING FLOWER AND LEAF COMBINATIONS may be achieved with a little trial and error. Some associations will readily suggest themselves, others will need to be worked at. Teaming copper with lime-green, purple with grey and orange with blue are just a few of the compositions to be tried. Equally successful are blue, white and silver or simply primrose and white.

Viola labradorica This moody little viola looks very effective when interplanted with silver leafed artemisias. 10 × 30cm/4in × 1ft

STAKING

Ensuring that taller-growing perennials will not collapse in wind and rain is vital if attractive borders are to be maintained.

Supporting stakes should be set around plants whilst growth is still at an early stage.

An alternative to ready-made stakes are hazel or birch twigs. Bamboo canes tied with twine will also provide adequate support. All supports will be hidden in a short while as foliage increases.

***Aquilegia* 'Magpie'** A sombre atmosphere is created by placing this unusual aquilegia amongst purple sage. 60 × 45cm/ 2 × 1½ft

◆ *Aquilegias come readily from seed but will frequently cross one with another.*

Viola cornuta alba Use this charming and understated viola to infill amongst other perennials. 10 × 30cm/ 4in × 1ft

Erysimum 'Bowles' Mauve'
This perennial wallflower looks splendid against a silver background.
60 × 60cm/2 × 2ft

Gillenia trifoliata A most graceful and unusual plant to bring life to otherwise dull areas. 1m x 60cm/3 x 2ft

Iris sibirica The lavender blue of this Siberian flag tones well with pale pinks. For moist soil. ◯, 60 × 60cm/2 × 2ft

Lychnis chalcedonica A difficult red to place outside a hot scheme. Look out for the double form.
1m × 45cm/3 × 1½ft

Thermopsis montana Straw-yellow flower closely resembles that of a lupin. The plant has a tendency to run. 75 × 75cm/2½ × 2½ft

Veronica austriaca 'Shirley Blue' Drift this sprawling plant throughout a yellow and blue border. ◯, 20 × 30cm/8in × 1ft

Alchemilla mollis (Lady's mantle) Lime-green flowers over clumps of slightly glaucous leaves which hold the raindrops in a most appealing manner.
60 × 60cm/2 × 2ft

Diascia vigilis Put this pretty pink with the silver-grey foliage of lamb's ears *Stachys byzantina* 'Silver Carpet'. ◯, 45 × 60cm/1½ x 2ft

Baptisia australis The false indigo is a worthwhile plant to seek out and include in a blue scheme. 75 × 60cm/2½ × 2ft

Geranium phaeum Named the mourning widow. Cut back after flowering to encourage a second show. ◑, 75 × 45cm/2½ × 1½ft

BEDDING OUT

RECENT YEARS HAVE SEEN A REVIVAL of formal bedding schemes where massed plants make for eye-catching displays. The large number of plants required can mostly be raised from seed. Informal use of bedding plants also provides some bright splashes during the duller months.

Nigella Love-in-the-mist creates an ephemeral effect when allowed to drift through the border.
○, 45cm/1½ft

Nemesia Easily grown, nemesia is quick to flower in a wide array of colours.
○, 30–45cm/1–1½ft

Limnanthes douglasii (Poached egg flower) Edge a border with this sunny little flower which is loved by bees. ○, 15cm/6in

Salvia splendens There is nothing understated about the many red varieties of this permanently popular annual. ○, 30cm/1ft

Nicotiana Intensely fragrant at dusk, nicotiana (the tobacco flower) should be grown near a path where its perfume may be appreciated.
○, 30–90 × 30–45cm/ 1–3 × 1--1½ft

Felicia amelloides Plant the blue marguerite in groups to fill any spaces left in sunny borders.
○, 45 × 30cm/1½ × 1ft

MANY OF THE PLANT COMBINATIONS used in parks and public gardens, where bedding out is a seasonal task, can readily be adapted to the beds and borders of the smaller garden. Alternatively, pots and tubs can be filled with dramatic results.

Petunia F1 hybrids will give a constant succession of flowers from planting out until the frosts.
○, 15–45cm/6in–1½ft

Heliotrope Somewhat less commonly used today than in the past, heliotrope (or cherry pie) is strongly perfumed. ○, 45cm/1½ft

Pelargonium Zonal pelargoniums are happiest in full sun and make ideal subjects for beds or containers.
○, 45cm/1½ft

◆ *Often commonly named geranium, pelargoniums will not withstand frost.*

45

A wonderful combination of tall foxgloves pushing through a bush of the hybrid musk rose 'Penelope' on the edge of woodland.

46

SOME PLANTS ARE LIKE OLD FRIENDS. Familiar, constant and reliable they have proved their worth time and time again. They are part of the garden tradition and it would be difficult to imagine flower borders without them.

***Rosa gallica* 'Camaieux'** The combination of white, pink, crimson in this old rose will excite comment. 1.5 × 1.2m/5 × 4ft

***Geranium endressii* 'Wargrave Pink'** This hardy geranium makes effective ground cover. 60 × 60cm/ 2 × 2ft

◆ *The majority of hardy geraniums will benefit from being cut hard back after flowering.*

Digitalis purpurea The foxglove is a splendid plant to include in a shady position at the back of the border. 1.2m × 30cm/4 × 1ft

Lilium martagon Of all the species this is possibly best known with its turban-shaped flowers. The form shown here is *L. m. album*. ◖ 1.5 × 30cm/5 × 1ft

Lupinus polyphyllus Russell lupins are amongst the brightest of the early summer flowers. ○, 1.2m × 45cm/4 × 1½ft

◆ *A number of distinct colours are in cultivation: 'Limelight', 'Vogue' and 'Magnificence'.*

***Nepeta* 'Six Hills Giant'** Deep blue flowers and silvery leaves make this a very attractive plant. ◑, 60 × 60cm/2 × 2ft

OLD-FASHIONED FLOWERS

***Paeonia lactiflora* 'Sarah Bernhardt'** Double, soft pink flowers with the appearance in texture of crumpled tissue paper. 1 × 1m/3 × 3ft

GROWING PEONIES

Peonies are suitable for planting in sun or light shade. Crowns should be placed fairly close to the surface of the soil. If placed too deeply, then they will flower less freely.

Peonies prefer rich, heavy, well-drained soil which remains moist during summer months. They will grow better if given some form of support.

They resent disturbance.

Polemonium reptans The blue Jacob's ladder will, if left, gently seed around. 30 × 45cm/1 × 1½ft

***Geranium pratense* 'Mrs Kendall Clark'** A charming geranium which fits into many colour schemes. 60 × 60cm/2 x 2ft

Lunaria annua Strictly speaking a biennial, honesty is most often grown for its pearly seed pods. ◑, 75 × 30cm/2½ × 1ft

Scabiosa caucasica The flowers of this scabious are a pretty addition to the early summer scene. ○, 60 × 60cm/2 × 2ft

***Centaurea montana* 'Alba'** This form of cornflower will respond to division every three years. 45 × 60cm/1½ × 2ft

Crambe cordifolia Wonderful sprays of frothy, scented white flowers for the back of the border. ○, 2 × 1.2m/6 × 4ft

Hesperis matronalis Although short-lived the scented sweet rocket will usually self-seed. ◑, 75 x 60cm/2½ x 2ft

Aquilegia vulgaris A true cottage-garden plant, the colombine has attractive grey-green leaves. ◑, 75 × 45cm/2½ × 1½ft

BROAD BEDS OF FLAG IRIS and long peony borders capture the imagination now. As flowers fade and dead heads are removed, attractive foliage maintains interest in terms of form and texture. It is worth keeping the flower beds tidy and neat so that shapes can be appreciated.

OLD-FASHIONED FLOWERS

Flag irises enjoy a situation where their creeping rhizomes can be sun-baked. Here they are shown with gladiolus.

◆ *Lift irises such as these and divide every few years.*

4. Midsummer

*Summer days bring warm, sunny hours.
Burgeoning flower borders reach peaks
of perfection.*

SUMMER SCENTS

CONTINUITY OF BLOOM

As the season progresses early-flowering plants, including many of the spring bulbs, will have finished blooming and have died down. To achieve continuity and a well furnished look, these gaps must be filled. In many cases the later-flowering perennials will reach maturity to obscure vacant spaces. Additionally annuals, such as centaurea, clarkia and the deliciously scented stocks, mathiola, can be introduced. These will flower right up until the first of the winter frosts.

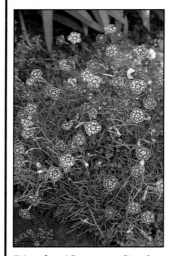

Dianthus **'Gravetye Gem'** All the pinks enjoy an open, free draining site. ○, E, 20 × 30cm/8in × 1ft

Dianthus **'Pike's Pink'** A delightful subject for the rock garden or front of border. ○, E, 15 × 15cm/ 6 × 6in

Iris graminea **(Plum tart iris)** Flowers, smelling of cooked plums, nestle well down amongst the leaves. ◑, 30cm × 30cm/1 × 1ft

Lilium candidum Heavily scented flowers in purest white make the Madonna lily an outstanding subject. ○, 1.2m/4ft

◆ *Lilies should not be allowed to dry out. Water well during dry weather.*

Lilium **'Uchida'** Charmingly marked. This lily would be equally at home in a container. ○, 1.2m/4ft

MIDSUMMER AIR IS PERFUMED WITH BEWITCHING SCENTS carried on gentle breezes. Bees murmur throughout long, dreamy days and borders are overrun with fragrant blooms. Now is the moment to linger, to delight in the riches of an unfolding, changing landscape.

Monarda **'Cambridge Scalet'** It is the leaves of the bergamots which are so strongly aromatic.
○, 1 × 1m/3 × 3ft

Origanum laevigatum. In common with most herbs, marjoram thrives in a sunny spot. 60 × 60cm/2 × 2ft

Lavandula No garden should be without generous clumps of sweet-smelling lavender. ○, 60 × 60cm+/2 × 2ft+

◆ *Clip lavenders hard back in the spring to retain healthy, vigorous plants.*

SUMMER SCENTS

Evening heightens the heady scent of lilies grown in the open ground or grouped in pots. Lavenders spill out onto paths, their fragrance familiar and nostalgic. Tobacco flowers release exotic aromas as twilight gathers.

Lathyrus odoratus is the original sweet pea. Over the years the range of colours has greatly increased. ○, 30cm–2.4m/1–8ft

CULTIVATING SWEET PEAS

Young plants should be set out in prepared soil containing plentiful amounts of compost or manure.

Train plants to grow up a supporting structure. In the border bean-sticks or bamboo canes are perfectly satisfactory.

Tie in tendrils to supports and water well in periods of dry weather. Remove all spent flowers to ensure a continuous succession of blooms.

Cosmos atrosanguineus (Chocolate cosmos) Unbelievably smelling of hot chocolate, this plant is a must. Suitable for a pot. ○, 75 × 45cm/2½ × 1½ft

Lathyrus rotundifolius Flowers of brick-red make this a most unusual perennial pea. 1.8m/6ft

Phlox **'Fujiyama'** A handsome plant with large heads of pure white which are pleasantly scented.
○, 1m × 75cm/3 × 2½ft

Phlox **'Norah Leigh'** Lilac flowers are carried above prettily variegated leaves.
○, 75 × 60cm/2½ × 2ft

Hemerocallis lilioasphodelus **(H. flava)** This day lily is scented. Removal of dead heads prolongs flowering.
75 × 75cm/2½ × 2½ft

Nicotiana The enticing fragrance of tobacco plants will fill an enclosed space.
○, 30–90 × 30–45cm/1–3 × 1–1½ft

◆ *Nicotiana is best treated as a half-hardy annual and raised from seed each year. It is shown here behind a mist of gypsophila.*

Mown grass acts as a quiet foil to a diversity
of flower tints. Taller growing phlox and
campanulas hold sway at the back of the
border. Mound-forming clumps and plants
which trail hug the ground to add intimacy
and variety.

CAREFULLY ORCHESTRATED BORDERS of complementary flowers and foliage are the outstanding feature of the season. Plants closely packed together bestow a wonderful sense of fullness and, on a practical note, deny weeds the opportunity for growth.

A LIVING TAPESTRY

***Rosa* 'Graham Thomas'**
This new English rose associates beautifully with deep blue delphinium. ○, 1.5 × 1m/5 × 3ft

***Alstroemeria* 'Ligtu Hybrids'** The eye is drawn towards the soft pink alstroemerias in this scheme. ○, 60 × 30cm/2 × 1ft

Geranium psilostemon and ***Geranium* 'Johnson's Blue'** These two hardy geraniums create a dramatic effect when placed together. 60 × 60cm/2 × 2ft

◆ *Bright colours are here toned down with the silver-leafed stachys.*

A Living Tapestry

Now is an ideal time in which to plan alterations to the flower garden. A critical look at the borders will show up those plants which perform badly, those which have outgrown their allocated space and those whose colours clash. Intended changes may be noted down in readiness for the autumn when plants may be lifted, divided and moved.

***Argyranthemum* 'Jamaica Primrose'** A most appealing tender marguerite for a warm spot. ○, 1 × 1m/ 3 × 3ft

Stachys macrantha is distinctive for its purplish-pink flowers. A good front-of-border plant. 45 × 45cm/1½ × 1½ft

Eryngium variifolium The steely blue flower-heads of this sea-holly are rounded and spiky. ○, 45 × 25cm/ 1½ft × 10in

Campanula poscharskyana This rockery campanula will quickly spread to cover a wide area. 25 × 60cm/ 10in × 2ft

Campanula pyramidalis A giant Canterbury bell. Plant this to tower through and above old roses. ○, 1.2m × 60cm/4 × 2ft

Lychnis coronaria A striking plant although the magenta flowers sometimes make it difficult to place. ○, 45 × 45cm/1½ × 1½ft

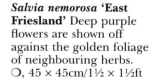

***Salvia nemorosa* 'East Friesland'** Deep purple flowers are shown off against the golden foliage of neighbouring herbs. ○, 45 × 45cm/1½ × 1½ft

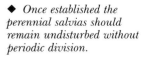

◆ *Once established the perennial salvias should remain undisturbed without periodic division.*

PLANTING IN BLOCKS OF COLOUR is a way of giving an effective structure to the herbaceous border. Whites, blues, lemons and creams on the outside edges; towards the centre pastel pinks to deeper shades of carmine, fiery reds and oranges crowned with purples and mauves.

A LIVING TAPESTRY

Thalictrum aquilegiifolium (Meadow rue) Fluffy pink flowers create a sense of lightness and airiness. 75 × 60cm/2½ × 2ft

Penstemon 'Chester Scarlet' There is nothing uncertain about this scarlet. Penstemons may be increased by taking cuttings. ○, 60 × 45cm/2 × 1½ft

Hemerocallis Clumps of red and orange day lilies convey the full heat of summer in this hot border. 1 × 1m/ 3 × 3ft

Acanthus spinosissimus Purple-tipped bracts in elegant spikes make this a plant of distinction. ○, 1.2m × 75cm/4 × 2½ft

Helichrysum italicum The curry plant shown with geraniums and catmint. ○, 60 × 60cm/2 × 2ft

◆ *Herbs need not be confined to the kitchen garden. They often make good association plants.*

A LIVING TAPESTRY

Successive flower displays are the result of much thought and effort. Combinations are carefully considered and awareness is given to leaf form as well as to the colour of individual blooms. Some factors cannot be judged, but if you know your plants and local conditions you can achieve spectacular results.

Astrantia major involucrata
Even as the flowers of the masterwort die they continue to look interesting. ◐, 60 × 60cm/2 × 2ft

Campanula lactiflora must be one of the mainstays of the summer border. 1.2m × 60cm/4 × 2ft

***Monarda didyma* 'Croftway Pink'** (Bergamot) Seen here against the violet-blue of nepeta, to good effect. 1m × 45cm/3 × 1½ft

Linum narbonense settles happily amongst the paving stones where its roots enjoy a cool run. ○, 45 × 30cm/ 1½ × 1ft

Geranium sanguineum striatum at the front of the border to give a full, informal effect. 30 × 45cm/ 1 × 1½ft

Eremurus bungei
Conspicuous foxtail lilies dominate plants in a border giving height and interest. ○, 1.5m × 60cm/5 × 2ft

***Geranium himalayense* 'Plenum'** Lilac double flowers ensure the popularity of this appealing plant. 60 × 60cm/2 × 2ft

Achillea filipendulina 'Gold Plate' Bold clumps of yarrow add form to a carefully planned hot border. ○, 1.5m × 60cm/ 5 × 2ft

◆ *The flat-heads of yarrow are effective when seen against a plant with spires of flowers, like salvia.*

DARE TO GROW DIASCIAS

These exceedingly pretty, mainly pink garden plants have increased in popularity in recent years. However, an undeserved reputation for tenderness precludes their inclusion in many garden schemes. Given moist conditions with good drainage to minimize winter wet, they should survive, particularly if cutting back is delayed until mid-spring. All are easy to propagate from basal cuttings.

Diascia rigescens Sprawling spikes of pink flowers will last throughout the summer. ○, 30 × 45cm/1 × 1½ft

Lysimachia punctata A colourful border plant but one with a tendency to spread beyond bounds. 75 × 75cm/2½ × 2½ft

Dictamnus albus purpureus Slow to establish but well worth taking trouble over. 60 × 60cm/2 × 2ft

Hemerocallis 'Bonanza' Deep yellow flowers which bloom much of the summer if dead headed. 1 × 1m/ 3 × 3ft

AMONGST THE LOVELIEST and most desirable of summer flowers are those which will not withstand frost. Less-hardy plants make excellent subjects for pots and containers. Grouped together on a terrace or beside a door they can form an attractive feature. Brugmansias, cannas and a phormium dominate this display.

Fuchsia **'Thalia'** Dark, velvet leaves show off many hanging trumpets of scarlet. Propagate from cuttings.
○, 45 × 45cm/1½ × 1½ft

Gazania South African daisies, available in a whole range of colours, make for an intense show.
○, 30 × 20cm/1ft × 8in

Brugmansia (Angel's trumpet, datura) An excellent plant for a pot. Here, the long, white hanging trumpets look coolly elegant. ○, 1.2 x 1m/4 x 3ft

Felicia amelloides The flowers of the blue marguerite are appealing when teamed with the palest of lemon yellows. ○, 45 x 30cm/1½ x 1ft

TENDER PERENNIALS

COMBAT COLD

Many of these tender perennials will survive the winter provided they are given a frost-free place. Grow them in pots throughout the colder months and then transfer to the open ground for the gardening season. Repot as the temperature falls.

Hedychium coccineum **'Tara'** Brilliant tangerine spikes contribute a feeling of hot, exotic climes to the summer border.
○, 1.2 × 1m/4 × 3ft

◆ *For a more subtle scheme, try* Hedychium flavescens *which is pale yellow and scented.*

TENDER PERENNIALS

Dahlia merckii A beautiful and graceful tuberous plant. Very different from the ordinary run of dahlias. ○, 90 × 60cm/3 × 2ft

SUMMER BULBS

In addition to this dahlia it is worth seeking out other bulbs for the mid-season. For something different try *Tigridia pavonia*, *Ixia* and the dwarf *Rhodohypoxis*.

Lobelia syphilitica These elegant blue spires would enhance most situations. Soil should be kept moist. 1.2m × 30cm/4 × 1ft

Gladiolus hybrid Possibly these tall, rather stiff flower spikes are at their best in a formal bedding scheme. ○, 1.2m × 30cm/4 × 1ft

Lobelia tupa Spectacular in flower. This lobelia requires really good drainage and protection from winter wet. ○, 1.2m × 30cm/4 × 1ft

Salvia discolor Absolutely outstanding. Indigo-black flowers above white-felted leaves. Keep frost free. ○, 60 × 30cm/2 × 1ft

Eucomis bicolor The quiet charm of the green-flowered pineapple plant requires a warm spot. ○, 45 × 60cm/1½ × 2ft

Salvia uliginosa Adds grace later in the summer. Protect new shoots of the bog sage from slugs. ○, 2m × 45cm/ 6 × 1½ft

Given a little protection, many of the plants thought likely to succumb to frost will come through a cold winter. A sheet of glass, dying ferns or bracken placed across the plant's crown is often enough to ensure survival.

Salvia patens The beautiful bright blue flowers are produced on the branches all summer to autumn. ○, 60 × 45cm/2 × 1½ft

Lobelia cardinalis 'Queen Victoria' Deep wine red leaves and stems and intense red flowers dominate this striking plant. ○, 90 × 30cm/3 × 1ft

◆ *Surprisingly this foliage and flower looks superb when set against orange.*

5. LATE SUMMER/ AUTUMN

Borders are ablaze with the rich hues of autumn as the Flower Garden moves into a new and thrilling season.

A LATE SHOW

As summer draws to a close the autumn flowers come into their own. Exciting kniphofias, fiery crocosmias and late-flowering salvias ensure an interesting and continuous display.

Dahlia **'Gerrie Hoek'** This intense pink associates well with pink Japanese anemones. ○, 60 × 60cm/ 2 × 2ft.

Crocosmia **'Lucifer'**, *Dahlia* **'Bishop of Llandaff'** Placed together these two late flowering plants bring excitement to the border. ○

◆ *Dahlia tubers should be lifted in the autumn and stored in a frost-free place.*

EASY TO GROW

Persicaria campanulata
Until the first frosts the red stems of this persicaria remain an outstanding feature at the back of the border. 1 × 1m/3 × 3ft.

AN HERBACEOUS CLEMATIS

Clematis heracleifolia Grow this non-climbing clematis for its sky blue, scented flowers. Delay cutting back and tidying the dead stems until the spring.
1m × 75cm/3 × 2½ft.

Kniphofia caulescens This striking poker has interesting grey-green, serrated leaves. ○,
1m × 60cm/3 × 2ft

Macleaya microcarpa Allow plenty of space for this dramatic perennial.
2 × 1m/6 × 3ft.

A Late Show

Glowing colours typify the time of year. A last rose ('Just Joey'), the flat yellow heads of achillea and generous clumps of crocosmias and dahlias maintain interest throughout the garden. In the foreground the crimson tassels of amaranthus (Love-lies-bleeding) elegantly sweep to the ground.

A LATE SHOW

***Dahlia* 'Grenadier'**
Tuberous dahlias dress up an end of season border. ○, 60 × 60cm/2 × 2ft.

TIDYING THE BORDERS

Frequent dead heading, the cutting down of spent plants and a light forking over of the ground keep the borders trim and in shape.

BOLDLY PLANTED CLUMPS of late-flowering perennials contribute a sense of drama to the borders. Far from fading, these autumn tints are rich, lustrous and full of purpose. Not least are the lovely cultivars of *Anemone hybrida*, the Japanese anemones.

WITHOUT EQUAL

Amongst the many available cultivars of ***Anemone hybrida*** are **'Hadspen Abundance'**, a deep purplish pink, **'Honorine Jobert'**, a large white, or **'Königin Charlotte'**, the best of the mid-pinks. 1.5m/5ft.

◆ *All the Japanese anemones have an extended flowering period. Cut back as the flowers fade.*

***Phygelius* × *rectus* 'Salmon Leap'** Treat this shrub as a perennial and cut back when the flowers are over. 1 × 1m/3 × 3ft.

Crinum powellii These beautiful, fragrant flowers are effective against a sunny wall. ○, 1m × 60cm/3 × 2ft.

◆ *Crinums are not difficult to grow but like a rich, well drained soil.*

Crocosmia 'Mount Usher' No garden should be without a selection of these perennials. ○, 60 × 30cm/ 2 × 1ft.

Kirengeshoma palmata A plant for moist ground close to water. ◑, 1m × 75cm/3 × 2½ft.

Fuchsia magellanica 'Gracilis Variegata' A graceful shrub with slender crimson-purple flowers. 75 × 75cm/2½ × 2½ft.

Agapanthus 'Loch Hope' Amongst the most magnificent of dark blue forms of African lily. ○, 1.2m × 75cm/4 × 2½ft.

Aconitum carmichaelii Roots of Monkshood, or Wolf's bane, are poisonous. 1.5m × 30cm/5 × 1ft.

Liriope muscari Tiny spikes of violet flowers are sometimes masked by the leaves. 30 × 45cm/1 × 1½ft.

ELEGANT AND UNUSUAL

Salvia × sylvestris 'Indigo' Mass together spires of this dark-flowered salvia for a beautiful and dramatic border statement. ○, 60 × 45cm/2 × 1½ft.

DAZZLING DAISIES

DAISY-TYPE FLOWERS dominate the late summer borders together with chrysanthemums and dahlias. These heavily petalled blooms enliven the last days of summer.

***Aster × frikartii* 'Mönch'** A long flowering period makes this a highly regarded daisy. ○, 75 × 45cm/2½ × 1½ft.

***Aster novi-belgii* 'Beechwood Charm'** Warm, vibrant flowers lighten drear days. ○, 1.2m × 45cm/4 × 1½ft.

***Aster novi-belgii* 'Goliath'** Regular division in spring results in freer flowering plants. ○, 1.2m × 45cm/ 4 × 1½ft.

A MINIATURE DAISY

***Aster thompsonii* 'Nanus'** Continuously in flower from mid-summer, this little aster is an invaluable garden plant. Place in a sunny spot and leave undisturbed. 45 × 25cm/1½ft × 10in.

***Aster novi-belgii* 'Lilac Time'**, ***Aster novi-belgii* 'Jenny'** These asters form a pleasing composition. ○

◆ *Taller growing asters require some form of staking. Hazel sticks are ideal.*

***Aster novi-belgii* 'Winston Churchill'** Silver-grey foliage is a marvellous foil for these flowers. ○, 75 × 45cm/2½ × 1½ft.

Michaelmas daisies are the grandees of all late flowering perennials. The flowers of the various species cover a broad spectrum and plants will prosper in most situations. In the past asters have been prone to mildew; many disease resistant strains are now available.

Clumps of dwarf asters hug the front of the border backed by those of taller stature. The introduction at intervals of white flowers helps to carry the eye forwards.

◆ *The scale of this late summer border may easily be adapted to fit a smaller space.*

DAZZLING DAISIES

ALONGSIDE ASTERS, dendranthema (as chrysanthemums have been renamed), heleniums, helianthus, and rudbeckias all contribute their daisy flowers to the warm glow of the autumnal borders. As the sun lowers so these tints are picked up and given greater intensity.

SHOW STOPPER

***Dendranthema* 'Corngold'**
Dendranthema such as this one make a bold statement. Specifically grown for cutting or show they are best given some form of protection from wind and rain. ○, 1.2m/4ft.

***Dendranthema* 'Ruby Mound'** Deep ruby red flowers are tightly packed together. ○, 1.2m/4ft.

◆ *An effective association is achieved by planting deep pink dendranthema with* **Sedum** **'Autumn Joy'**.

***Dendranthema* 'Nathalie'**
Named cultivars are the result of much crossing and recrossing. 90cm/3ft.

***Arctotis* × *hybrida* 'Wine'**
Treat this South African daisy as an annual in colder areas. ○, 60cm/2ft.

![main image of Rudbeckia flowers]

Rudbeckia fulgida **'Goldsturm'** These prolific yellow daisies with their black central cones seem to last for all time. Dead-heading prolongs the flowering season. ○, 75 × 45cm/ 2½ × 1½ft.

◆ *Partner* **'Goldsturm'** *with the purple daisy heads of the cone flower* **Echinacea purpurea**.

FRONT OF BORDER

Inula barbata A cheerful little subject to tuck in amongst other flowers. Petals are an unusual light, greenish yellow. ○, 60 × 45cm/2 × 1½ft.

Helianthus **'Monarch'** Brilliant yellow sunflowers soar skywards above rough foliage. ○, 2.1 × 1m/ 7 × 3ft.

◆ *Grown from seed sunflowers are great favourites with children.*

Helenium **'Moerheim Beauty'** Easily grown perennial with rich mahogany flowers. ○, 1m × 60cm/3 × 2ft.

AS THE GARDENING YEAR DRAWS TO A CLOSE, and thoughts once more turn to spring, there is still much in the flower garden to attract attention and excite interest.

Schizostylis coccinea alba In cold areas give the crowns some over-winter protection. 60 × 30cm/ 2 × 1ft

Schizostylis coccinea 'Sunrise' Kaffir lilies continue to bloom even in low temperatures. 60 × 30cm/2 × 1ft

Sedum 'Autumn Joy' Butterflies love this sedum which remains pleasing throughout the winter. ○, 60 × 60cm/2 × 2ft

Sedum 'Ruby Glow' Crimson flowers quietly fade as the year progresses. ○, 30 × 30cm/1 × 1ft

Colchicum speciosum
Planted in drifts under shrubs or trees, or in grass, there are few more attractive autumnal displays. ○, 20 × 20cm/ 8 × 8in

Enjoying partial shade, many forms of **Tricyrtis**, toad lily, form elegant clumps through the first fallen leaves.
60 × 45cm/2 × 1½ft

Nerine bowdenii These showy South African bulbs are reliably hardy.
○, 45 × 20cm/1½ft × 8in

◆ *When planting, place bulbs on a little horticultural grit to improve drainage.*